BEHIND THE CAMERA

Ciaran Murtagh

Illustrated by **Alex Paterson**

OXFORD
UNIVERSITY PRESS

Contents

Getting Started

So, you want to make a great kids' TV show? I have written for shows like *Mr Bean* and *Shaun the Sheep*, and I know just how hard it can be. First you need a great idea for a show, just like these.

Children's TV comes in all shapes and sizes. If you've got a great idea, there's room for you too. Couldn't be simpler, right? Wrong!

Making a great TV programme is like making a great cake. You need lots of ingredients, mixed in just the right way, to create something special.

If you get it right, your programme will be loved forever. If you get it wrong, your programme won't even make it on to the screen.

Imagine your TV idea is a drama. Everyone loves a good drama, but you'll need some help to turn it into a great TV programme. Luckily, I know just the people to ask!

The Producer

A producer guides a TV programme through every stage, from first idea to final **broadcast**.

Key skills

Organized, reliable

The producer is usually the first person involved in making a TV programme. They may have had the idea for the programme, or they may have been part of a team that thought up the idea. They find the best people to turn that idea into reality. They make sure that everyone knows what they have to do and when.

When the TV programme has been made, their job isn't finished – they have to start planning the next one!

If it sounds like a hard job, that's because it is!

The Writer

This is where I come in. A writer turns an idea for a TV programme into a script. The writer creates the stories and characters.

Key Skills

Creative, good communicator

It's the writer's job to turn an idea for a TV show into a story that viewers will love. Sometimes the writer approaches a producer with an idea. Sometimes the producer approaches the writer with an idea. Either way, the writer has to turn that idea into a script.

The writer may have to decide what **genre** to write in:

I've been expecting you!

Horror?

I've been expecting you!

Comedy?

I've been expecting you!

Action?

They may also have to decide the best way to tell the story – with cartoons, puppets or actors.

Animation

Once a script has been written, you could bring it to life with **animation**. In the past, cartoons were drawn by hand. Individual pictures were drawn and shown very quickly, one after the other. This makes it look like a moving image.

Today, cartoons can still be drawn by hand, but they are more often drawn on a computer.

The person who creates these cartoons is called an **animator**.

Animated films don't always have to be drawn. Puppets, clay models and objects can be turned into animations too. This way of filming is called 'stop-motion'.

The stop-motion animator stops the camera often to move objects a tiny amount. When the film is played the objects look like they are moving.

Once an animated film has been made, actors bring the characters to life with a voice-over.

The voice-over artists speak the characters' words and make them sound real. Then the animators make the characters' mouths match the words.

Live Action

You might want to use actors instead of animation. When actors are used in a TV programme it is called **live action**.

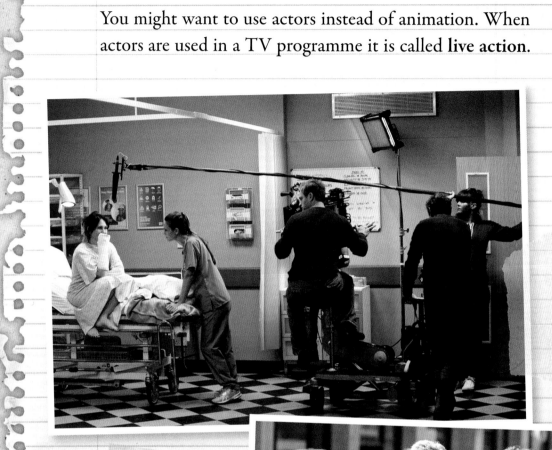

It's important to find the right actor for the right character! So how do you do this?

Is your character male or female?

How old?

How tall?

Do they have a beard?

Once you know this information, you can hold an **audition**.

In an audition, the producer, writer and director will ask different actors to read the parts for each character. They find the best actor to play every character.

The Director

The director is in charge of turning the script into a TV programme.

Key Skills

Strong leader, calm, creative

It's a director's job to turn the writer's script into images and sounds on the screen. To make a TV programme, you need many different people with many different skills. The director makes sure that all these people work together to make the best TV show possible.

A TV **set** can be a very busy place. The director is in charge of how every **shot** will look, so they have to be clear about what they want people to do.

Set, Props, Costume, Make-up

Before you start filming, you need to know where you're filming and how everyone and everything will look. These are the people who can help you.

SET DESIGNER

Are you going to be filming in a **studio** or **on location**? The set **designer** will find, or make, the right place and make everything look just right.

PROPS PEOPLE

Props is short for 'properties' – this means anything which is seen on the set. Do you need an exploding monster's head or a yellow teapot? They can find it for you – or make it.

COSTUME DESIGNER

Does your character need a queen's crown or a firefighter's safety jacket? The costume designer will get it for you. If they can't get it, they'll make it.

MAKE-UP ARTIST

These people are masters of the make-up brush. Do you want your actor to look glamorous or like an alien? They can make it happen!

Lights, Camera ... Action!

The director keeps everything moving with detailed instructions.

The camera person records everything that happens.

So you've got your script, you've got your actors, you even know what everyone is wearing! It's time for lights, camera ... action!

The lighting person makes sure that everyone can see the action.

Actors bring the script to life.

The sound person records every word spoken on set. They may use a microphone held above the actors, or there may be microphones hidden around the set and in actors' costumes.

Editing and Special Effects

So your TV programme has been filmed – now, is it ready? No!

THE EDITOR
The editor puts the TV programme together, after it's been filmed.

Key Skills
Attention to detail, techno whizz

The editor puts all the bits of your TV show together and decides which camera shots to use to tell the story.

SPECIAL EFFECTS

Your TV programme has been written, directed, acted, filmed and edited – now, is it ready? Not quite! Some things can't be filmed! It's time to add special effects.

Special effects change the way the programme appears or sounds. Do you want to add an explosion or a flying fairy – or both?

You've done it!

So there you have it. Your TV programme is ready to go!
The only thing left to do is to get ready for the awards party! When you get your award, don't forget to thank everyone who helped. Most importantly, don't forget to thank me for getting you started in the first place!

Glossary

animation: making films from still pictures, puppets or models so they appear to move

animator: a person who creates images that make still characters look like they are moving

audition: an interview to see if a performer is suitable to act as a character

broadcast: to transmit a programme on a TV or radio

designer: someone who creates costumes or sets to be used on TV, film or stage

genre: a style of TV programme, e.g. horror, comedy, drama

live action: action involving filming real people or animals

on location: when a film is filmed in natural surroundings, not in a studio

script: the text of a TV show, play, film or radio programme

set: the background in a TV programme, film or play

shot: a photograph or piece of film

stop-motion: a way of filming where the camera is stopped and started with objects moved a tiny amount each time the camera stops, to make models or puppets look like they are moving

studio: a room or set of rooms where TV programmes are made

voice-over: spoken material for a film or a TV programme

Index

About the Author

Hello, my name is Ciaran and I live in London. I have written several books for children and I write lots of children's TV shows including *Shaun the Sheep*, *The Amazing World of Gumball* and *Mr Bean*. I also appear as a performing prisoner on the TV show *The Slammer*.

Behind the Camera has been great fun to write. Whenever you watch a TV programme there are lots of people you don't see on screen who helped to make it happen. I've enjoyed giving them a little limelight and helping you understand how the TV you love is made.

Greg Foot, Series Editor

I've loved science ever since the day I took my papier mâché volcano into school. I filled it with far too much baking powder, vinegar and red food colouring, and WHOOSH! I covered the classroom ceiling in red goo. Now I've got the best job in the world: I present TV shows for the BBC, answer kids' science questions on YouTube, and make huge explosions on stage at festivals!

Working on TreeTops inFact has been great fun. There are so many brilliant books, and guess what ... they're all packed full of awesome facts! What's your favourite?